"WE REMEMBER D-DAY"

British and American Eye-Witness Accounts from the Dart Area to Normandy

CW01508530

INTRODUCTION

On June 3rd, 1944 when 485 ships and landing craft left the Dart estuary to join the vast invasion forces which were to attack Normandy three days later it was the culmination of over a year's planning and rehearsals, many of which had been carried out in the river and the surrounding countryside.

This book gathers together the memories of a cross section of those who were involved, one way or another. They include the civilians who lived beside the Dart, the British servicemen and women who came here to take part in the great preparations, the people of the South Hams who were turned out of their homes and farms to allow practice landings to take place on Slapton beach, and the American and Allied forces who were to fill the landing craft for the assault on the great day.

Even after fifty years their memories are vivid. Some kept diaries surreptitiously at the time or wrote their thoughts in letters home. All of them were aware at the time that they were playing a part in the biggest operation of the war - one which would lead, if successful, to the defeat of Germany. Everyone had their own private feelings. Those taking part did not know if they would survive the battle. Those left behind feared for their loved ones, many of whom did not come back.

This then is not an official history but a collection of personal stories about a dramatic period of the war by those who were actually there.

Dartmouth History Research Group

Chapter 1
The Planning of Operation Overlord

Before the Allied forces could hope to succeed in launching an invasion force from Britain, code-named OVERLORD, against the heavily fortified French coast, three preliminary things were essential. First, they had to win the Battle of the Atlantic so that the Navy could ensure the safe passage of the huge numbers of landing craft across the Channel. Second, they had to defeat the Luftwaffe to prevent it attacking the fleet and troops on the initial assault. Third, there had to be a Deception Plan to prevent the Germans concentrating all their defences on the chosen assault area and to make them think it was elsewhere. The Germans had for several years been building up the "Atlantic Wall" from Brittany to the Netherlands.

In tactical terms, Churchill himself had stressed the need to develop floating breakwaters and piers, code-named "Mulberry," a harbour which could be placed off any beach without the need to capture an existing port which the Germans would obviously destroy to prevent its use. A pipe-line to carry fuel across the Channel - "Pluto" - would also be needed. In Britain and America large numbers of landing craft were built, specially designed to carry troops, artillery, tanks and so on.

The Allied High Command had secretly decided that of the various options for landing in France, the area between the Cherbourg peninsula and the River Orne was to be the one chosen. There were beaches suitable for troop landings and RAF reconnaissance photos showed that the defences there were less developed than in other areas which the Germans expected to be attacked. However, inland there was the disadvantage that this is "Bocage" country, with narrow winding lanes and high hedgerows and, in one area, behind the code-named "Utah" beach, there was a lake or swampy area which could be flooded.

This part of France greatly resembled Slapton Sands in Devon with its raised beach, the Ley behind it, and the villages linked by narrow lanes and high hedges. It had already, in 1938, been used by Montgomery as a place on which to practice landing troops from the sea. Like all the other South coast areas, it had been closed to the public since the beginning of the war so that it could be defended against a possible German landing. Now it was to be used to simulate Allied landings in France.

An aerial view of Slapton Sands with the Ley behind.

Chapter 2
Training in Dartmouth Royal Naval College Buildings, 1943

By January of 1943 the Cadets at Britannia Royal Naval College had been evacuated to Cheshire. The college became the base for Combined Operations forces who trained on landing craft which went out from the Dart to practice landing on Slapton beach. At this time the College was known as HMS Dartmouth III, but on July 19th it was re-named HMS Effingham.

Richard Davies recalls:

"I joined the Navy in February 1943 and served in HMS Collingwood and became a cox'n. We came to Dartmouth to finish training on landing craft, at the College. I came in May 1943, and we stayed here about three months. We trained at Slapton in handling landing craft. The craft I trained on would hold 32 fully equipped soldiers. These were the same size as those that went across on D-Day. They had larger craft for the tanks, lorries, etc. The craft I trained on would carry a small vehicle if they wanted to. I trained on LCVs (Landing Craft Vehicles), LCAs (Landing Craft Assault) and one part of the year I did go on the LCTs, that is the Landing Craft Tank. I did pass out on them as well. I'd got my own landing craft, there was 12 in the flotilla, and my job was to take the troops from embarkation and deposit them on the beaches. We picked them up from the land, went out to sea, pretended we were going to France, turned round and came back, and landed them on the beaches."

So far these exercises had been done without using live ammunition.

Royal Naval exercises with landing craft on Blackpool beach, Spring 1943.

Chapter 3
The Evacuation of the Slapton Area

However, by the autumn of 1943 it was decided that Slapton beach would become a major practice area for the D-Day landings, using live ammunition and recreating the defences likely to be put up by the Germans on any beach to be attacked. The intention was to simulate real battle conditions for troops without any such experience. Since the barrage of artillery from the ships was bound to cause extensive damage to the whole area under attack, the entire population of the area from Torcross to Blackpool Sands, and inland for about ten miles was to be evacuated.

The Authorities received the news direct from the Cabinet with considerable alarm. How were they to tell the inhabitants, about 3,000 people, that they were to be moved out of their homes, shops and farms at short notice for an indefinite period? And what was to happen to their empty property with all this bombardment?

The Western Morning News reported that the Lord Lieutenant of Devon, Lord Fortescue, on November 12th, 1943 presided over a meeting in East Allington village church to inform the villagers of the decision. The Regional Commissioner Sir Hugh Ellis told them:

"I have never had a task put upon me such as I have now to do. There are 840 households, over 200 farms, and many thousand head of good stock, and we have been asked to do this so that the Services may take over and begin practice by January 1st. The case against taking up that area, a case for the valuable agricultural property, the case for the upsetting of their lives; all that had been put before the Ministers."

However, Sir Hugh quoted from a speech by Winston Churchill, that 1944 would see the climax of the war and would see the greatest sacrifice of life.

"Neither the men who would have to take part in operations, nor their relations and friends, would want them to go in without every possible training, and they had also to try out the weapons and craft they were going to use. They would have to practice every day as long as God gave them fine weather. That was why residents were being asked to surrender their land to permit the practice to take place."

A U.S. Officer then said that "battle inoculation would save many lives, and he knew that whatever the hardships caused by the move they would be offset by the lives of American and British soldiers that would be saved when the time came, from the lessons they were going to learn in that area."

The villagers had to be out by December 20th - five days before Christmas. Freda Widger, a farmer's daughter in Slapton, remembers how the villagers there heard about this:

"My mother's cousin lived at the Round House at Slapton - they had Army men billeted on them, and when rumours circulated that we were to be evacuated even the Army men said: 'Impossible - they could not possibly clear out such a big area.' All of a sudden we had a notice that

Dotted lines show the area of the South Hams evacuated to enable practices by Allied Forces using live ammunition to be carried out.

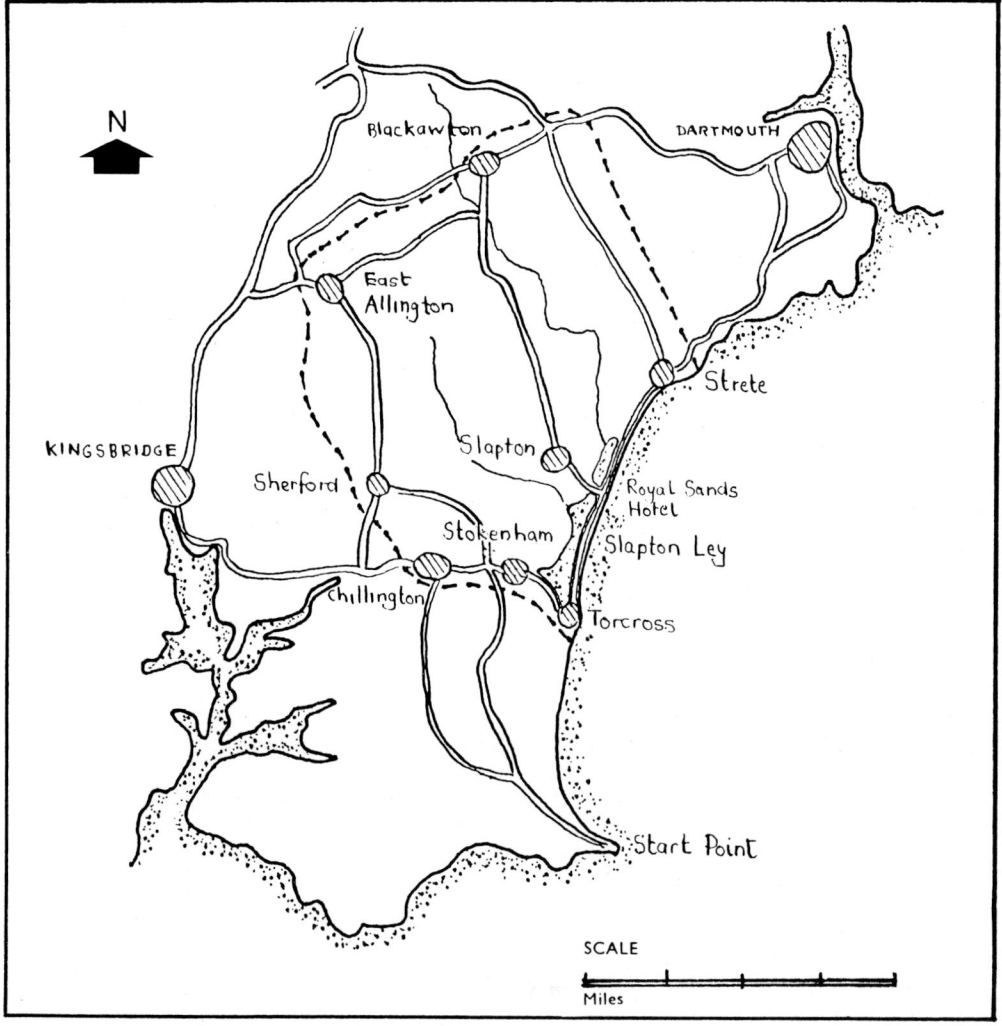

there was to be a meeting in the village hall, the villagers had to attend, and we were told we had six weeks to clear out. I remember the meeting well. I was about 22 or 23. Everyone was up in arms. One old man wouldn't go. We all thought it was going to be for a month, perhaps six weeks. We did not realise it was going to be for eleven or twelve months. We did not realise that everything would have to go, we thought we were going for a holiday, more or less.

"The thing was to find somewhere to go. We supplied part of the village with milk, we had cows, everybody could not sell everything. There was nobody to buy it. What could you do with your animals? I went with my father - he did not drive - to a cousin at Totnes to see if he could help us. He saw a farmer at Empston valley and said, 'Well they've got no animals, just let the grass, I'll ring them and see if they could accommodate you.' It was an awful farm, right down by the railway line and the river at Littlehempston. They said 'yes', mother and father could have two bedrooms in the house and they could share the kitchen, and they could have some of their animals there.

"I could go with my future husband's family near Hallsands. I would take some of the poultry with me, and they would have some of the bullocks, and my future husband spent two or three weeks coming over with tractor and trailer taking mangolds, hay and stuff to feed the bullocks that they took. They could not spare their feed for our bullocks. We had a friend the other side of Blackawton who took some as well. We took the rest to Totnes. We had to sell the cows as nobody wanted the milk. They kept one for themselves, the rest had to go. My mother was very unhappy; she was born in the village and had always lived there. We went out from there a fortnight before Christmas - it was really a traumatic time to go out just before Christmas. We were about the last to leave as we were supplying the village with milk. Everybody depended on us."

Pearl Rogers, her brother Terence, and Basil Mitchelmore were children when the Americans arrived in Slapton at the end of November. Like all children, they flocked around the Yanks and were rewarded with sweets and chewing gum.

American trucks and troops arrived in Slapton Village, beside the Chantry, in November 1943. Basil Mitchelmore and Terence Rogers, like most children, found them a good source of sweets and chewing gum.

Pearl's father, Frank Rogers, had the butchers shop in Slapton which had to close when they left. There was no compensation given for the loss of income from the business for nearly a year. Her father got a job on a farm and was then called up as he no longer ran his own business. When they returned to Slapton her mother had to run the butchers shop by herself.

"I remember going with my mother to look for somewhere to rent. At one house in Brixham the lady took one look at my brother and me and slammed the door in our face - she did not want children! For some, the thought of moving out of the village they had lived in for over 80 years was just too much. One old couple, Mr. and Mrs Jarvis, refused to look for anywhere and in the end said: 'We're coming with you, Frank.' They were old friends, but not related. So we rented a larger house in West Buckland, to have room for the old couple. However, Mrs Jarvis died before we left, and Mr. Jarvis died soon after the Christmas. People forget the shock to the old of leaving the village where they had lived all their lives. They could not even be buried in their native village."

Dick Rushton volunteered to drive the villagers to their new homes. He remembers that the weather that November was almost endlessly wet, making a difficult job even more dreary. The lanes were muddy and even more churned up than usual as the Americans arrived with their heavy lorries. There were so many traffic jams as vehicles met head on in the narrow lanes that soon a one way system was devised. Some of the old people he drove were completely numb with shock. Sometimes, when they arrived, the relatives who had said they could stay with them changed their minds and refused to have them. He took one couple to four different addresses on four days before they would settle.

Pearl Rogers watched her father Frank (on right) load his butcher's table into a van when they had to leave their butcher's shop in Slapton in December 1943. Helping him, in the striped apron, was Mr Edward Hannaford, another butcher from Torcross.

A steam tractor towing a threshing machine from a South Hams farm when it was evacuated to make way for battle training on Slapton beach.

Chapter 4
The Americans take over the Royal Naval College

Among the first to know that the American arrival was imminent was the Post Office. Young Eric Pillar, then a messenger, was told by the Post Master:

"We've got some mail come for some American forces that are coming here. Go down and collect it from the Station."

"So I went off with a wheelbarrow, a sort of hand truck, down the steeply sloping long ramp to the old waiting room at the bottom of the station pontoon. It happened to be low tide. I got to the platform and each side was up to the ceiling with huge mailbags, twice the weight of the regulations for this country. There was me with my wheelbarrow. The fellow there said: 'We've got another lot like this at Kingswear.'"

It was late one dark evening in December 1943 when the first American ships arrived in the Dart. Eric describes the scene:

"They came in all lit up - and this was when we were still having air raids, so blackout regulations were strict. There was an air raid warning in progress at the time! The Royal Navy in their headquarters on the Embankment used loud hailers to shout at them to douse their lights, but to no avail. Only after they fired a burst of tracer bullets across the top of them did the lights go out."

Once they had arrived, the Americans made themselves at home. Wren Officer Ruth Bryant writes:

"Soon there was an American sentry at the College gate, and their large ships, blaring out music, unloaded their stores on the quayside."

But worse was to come. Eric Barker, the comedian, in HMS Effingham at the Royal Naval College at the time, wrote:

"The Yankees arrived in Dartmouth to take over. It put years on the Royal Navy Officers, who had been brought up in the place. I was sorry for the Commander......There was a quarter-deck at Dartmouth which was his pride and joy. Any man who failed to salute it was mercilessly dealt with. At the far end was a statue of His Majesty King George V with a telescope under his arm, and every day a fatigue party was detailed to polish him.

"The first thing the Yankees did was to use the quarter-deck as a store for dozens of packing cases labelled, 'Lucky Strike Cigarettes.' The final blow for the poor Commander came one day on the ruins of the quarter-deck when a huge Negro put a cigar in his mouth and lit it with a match which he struck on the statue of His Late Britannic Majesty."

HMS Effingham was moved out of the College to make way for the Americans at the end of December.

Britannia Royal Naval College became the Headquarters of the US Navy.

The statue of H.M. King George V on the quarter-deck at the Royal Naval College.

Chapter 5
The Locals' View of the Yankee Invasion

American soldiers on a Sherman tank on the Embankment, Dartmouth. It was adapted to operate in six feet of water. Behind, the "Ship in Dock" inn and nissen huts on Coronation Park.

Brian Bovey of Kingswear, then thirteen, was one of a gang of boys who found the newcomers both interesting and rewarding:

"There were no Americans billeted in Kingswear. The nearest were towards Hillhead, by some woods, coming from Paignton just before Hillhead garage. The blacks were one side, the whites on the other. They were laying a pipeline from Newton Abbot to Plymouth. These blacks were literally slaves to the whites."

It must be remembered that few Devon people had ever met a Negro, and were quite unaware of the segregation practised in the States until they saw it with their own eyes. Mrs Dawson, then a schoolgirl, remembers:

"A lot of Americans lived up in the College. There was an Army Camp at the top of the hill - possibly where the Park and Ride is now - where they had a camp for the negroes and one for the whites. They kept them separate. They came into town occasionally. At our Methodist Chapel, with the aid of the Flavel ladies we had a canteen in the top room. My Gran was in charge of the Methodists so I used to go with her and had a whale of a time. They were extremely friendly, the Negroes even more so. They were like gentle giants to me, as I was just a little girl at the time and they always seemed so big to me."

Everyone remembers how generous the Americans were with their sweets and spare food - the British who had been rationed since 1939, though not starving, had not seen luxuries for years. Despite orders not to upset the

rationing system by giving away food, ways were found to slip it to the locals. Mrs Dawson's father worked on the tug, Portway, which towed landing craft about for the Americans. She remembers:

"The Americans were not allowed to give things away but if they were going out to drop them overboard and the Portway was with them, they would surreptitiously hand it over. We had tins of their lovely jam."

Brian Bovey and his gang of friends ... "soon found that we were onto a good thing. We were always up there scrounging things, especially cigarettes - we lads all smoked like chimneys: Camels, Chesterfields, Lucky Strike. Food? Oh yes, the game was at weekends to go up the footpath from Kingswear to the Higher Ferry and you could pick up enough food to last you for the weekend. When they were loading up their landing craft, if the British dropped a tin of Spam they would say: 'Get it!' But the Americans often dropped whole boxes, waterproof boxes, and just left them. We would fish them out. Then there were the K-rations, coated with candle wax, they would often be floating in the river. In them were cigarettes, gum, malted tablets, tin of coffee, food in tablet form. You could always pick up life jackets, and half the people were wearing American jackets, 'bum freezers' they called them, and denims and the little white hats. The river was pretty solid with craft."

However, the giving was often a two way process. Peter Clare whose family were living in Dittisham recalls:

"My father grew all sorts of fresh lettuces in his garden, and thought these Yankee boys might like some, and maybe give us a bit of meat as they always had far more of anything than we had. They weren't supposed to take anything like this. He went out on my 8-foot rowing boat, Sambo, to these ships. There were patrol boats going up and down the river and strictly no one was allowed to go on the river or approach these vessels. The old man used to watch the patrol boat come up and go away, then he would row out and shout, 'Want any fresh vegetables?' Of course they liked fresh food after all those tins and they took quite a bit. They would say to my father, 'What do you want Pop?' In the end the boat would be loaded up with cigarettes, tins, this and that, in no time at all. Later he got to know the Captains of one or two of these vessels, and invited them back to our cottage for a bit of home life. When D-Day came and all the ships left my boat, Sambo, disappeared too - I believe they took it with them to Normandy!"

Brian Bovey describes how Coronation Park became a ship repair yard, working night and day on the landing craft. "They used to go on about us showing a light, but you should have seen the lights there. There were arc lights on all night - they only put them out when the air raid siren went." Since there was no such warning for the two worst raids on Dartmouth and Noss shipyard, that was not much comfort for the locals.

With so many Americans arriving in the town, in addition to the British and French forces already here, there was an acute shortage of girls which led to some friction at times. Brian Ridalls remembers how, at the age of 16 or so, he and the other Army Cadets used to organise dances in the Guildhall:

"There were British Commandos who started here in Dartmouth; they trained up at the college. I remember one fellow I knew very well. He was a Sergeant P.T.I. and had been a professional boxer before the war. They used to say

A US truck crossing the re-inforced bridge over the entrance to the Boatfloat, with the Quay and Castle Hotel behind. A small landing craft is passing in the river.

Coronation Park was filled with nissen huts, used to repair and service landing craft.

about him: 'When the invasion comes, God help the Germans.' These soldiers and sailors had always been coming to our dances, and suddenly these Americans turned up. I can remember one particular dance, these Americans always used to rub us up the wrong way because they had more money than we had, and they were pinching all the girls. There were only about 8 or 9 of these Commandos, and 20 or 30 of these Americans, and the soldiers got so fed up they threw these Americans out. I can see it now: there were two commandos at the top of the stairs, two down the bottom, two out by the door, and the rest in the hall getting hold of these Yanks, getting them to the top of the stairs where two were throwing them down the stairs and the other two were throwing them out."

Wren Margaret Blackwell confirmed that the Englishmen were "completely put out by the obviously compelling and successful technique of the Americans with the opposite sex." Americans were by nature very friendly and hospitable, as she herself found:

"I strolled up to Dartmouth College to a 'Wienie Roast.' Not having any idea what this was, I went to find out. It was a lovely fresh May evening, and the College grounds are really beautiful, just like a huge park. There under the trees was an open fire and on it were being grilled pieces of steak, - heaven knows where they got the steak but get it they did. Three trestle tables skirted the fire, where people stood or sat between dances. Dancing was in the hall inside. The steak was put in a split roll and you 'dug in' for pickles, etc. and there was coffee. It was such an easy, friendly affair and you could tell that you would be just as welcome any time you happened to 'blow by.'"

The appearance of the town altered. The whole Embankment and Coronation Park area was barred to anyone without a special pass. Brian Ridalls describes

what happened:

"They built out the Embankment with ramps between the double steps and Coronation Park. There were three slipways into the river. The ships came in alongside the slipway and these ramps were for the tanks to go onto them. They were these great big American LSTs (Landing Ship Tanks), about 300 feet long, with huge guns on the front and the back. The tanks went on into the bow of the ship and the troops went out on the scaffolding ramps onto the ship."

To reach the Embankment, as College Way had not yet been built, all the vehicles had to come down narrow Victoria Road and to pass the Butterwalk - already badly shaken by the bomb which had destroyed the corner of Foss Street and Duke Street in February 1943 - and then straight through the Royal Avenue Gardens. Brian Ridalls again:

"I can remember scores and scores of lorries and tanks coming down Victoria Road. Before the recent alterations to the Royal Avenue Gardens there was a reinforced concrete path across it from the Embankment to the Quay where the telephone kiosks are on the corner of the Boatfloat. The old bridge, made in the 17th century, was still there under the road when they filled in the old Pool in the 19th century and they had just covered it up. One day when a Sherman tank was crossing it just disappeared into a hole. After that the Yanks filled it in and put a reinforced concrete road all the way out to the Embankment. Now it is all covered with tiles since about two years ago."

Repair grids were built at Lower Noss Point and landing facilities up beyond Dittisham and by Waddeton Court, where U.S. troops were to join the landing craft from the Torbay side of the river.

Slipways were built out from the Embankment to enable the large LSTs to load up with vehicles and tanks.

Chapter 6
More realistic practices on Slapton Beach

British RN landing craft No. 228 on an exercise on Slapton beach, Spring 1944. Troops would be landed where they had to negotiate beach obstacles similar to those in France and live ammunition was used.

Meanwhile, practices increased on Slapton beach - at first with British landing craft transporting American troops there. Leading Seaman Jim George, a Cox'n on landing craft, recalls being trained at Dartmouth from late 1943 up until the final embarkation in June 1944:

"I was sent to the Naval College at Dartmouth. There were about 350 sailors and all our boats were tied up alongside the wall in the river Dart. There were LCMs, which could carry a three-ton truck, LCVPs for vehicles and personnel, and LCAs, small assault craft which you could run up on a beach. There were four to five hundred various boats, all in Dartmouth at the one time. They were tied up 3 or 4 deep alongside the wall from the Dartmouth railway station right up as far as you could go. That was the small craft. The larger craft, the LCTs and LSTs, (Landing Craft Tanks and Landing Ship Tanks), were moored in mid-river as far as you could see.

"In the morning we would see which boat we would go in - it did not matter which boat, as we belonged to a flotilla - known by numbers. You would go down to the dockside and be told; 'get in that boat or that boat.' We would pick up the troops, mostly American but sometimes British. Then we'd go out to sea, turn right and go to Slapton. I was the Cox'n - I was a leading seaman at the time, like a Corporal, in charge of the boat. There would be an Officer in charge of three or four.

"On ordinary days, the Commander of the Flotilla would hoist different flags for you to take up different formations, e.g., single file, or four at a time. We used to run onto the beach, throw down a kedge anchor, hit the beach, put down another anchor to hold the boat in. It was quite an interesting life but I wouldn't recommend it! On the smaller exercises no one was firing at us from the shore, but on the bigger ones they used live ammunition and there were casualties - none near me. Once we had carried the troops and they had gone ashore we had to clear the beach. There were officers on the beach like traffic wardens and they would shout to you to get away."

The American troops who took part in these attacks did not realise that the area they were attacking would ever be inhabited again. Staff Sergeant Bernard Krein of the 8th Infantry, 4th Division, wrote about it in his book, "Once Around the Block":

"The United States government bought an entire village along the coast, as close a replica as one we will have to fight through on the day of the invasion. Houses, stores, barns, hedges and a school. All that was missing was the people, their furniture and their pets. We attacked that village for two weeks, from the land and from the sea. We blew up houses, tore down boundary walls, threw grenades into windows, set and activated booby traps to see their deadly effects.... and on the fourth day an order came down from Division for us to take it easy on the village as the U.S. government was going to have to restore this once peaceful place. When the request was read to us at the

US landing ships 525 and 427, with covering barrage balloon, discharging troops on Slapton beach for an exercise, Spring 1944.

A painting by Com. Dwight Shepler, USNR, of an attack on Slapton beach using live ammunition. Tanks can be seen coming out of the water, troops are advancing up the beach, and naval bombardment causes explosions with clouds of smoke on the horizon.

beginning of another wet run, we really tore up the place .....NOW they are telling us to take it easy? A bit too late for that, they trained us well....'Don't knock the doors off the hinges ..... we're going to knock the houses off the doors.'"

Canadians at Slapton Beach

Not only the Americans and British but also Canadians used Slapton for practice runs. Lt. Peter Wyatt, RN, serving in HMS Waveney, was involved in training Assault Force J2, in conjunction with the 9th Canadian Brigade under Brigadier Blackadder, which was later to land on Juno beach at Courseulles. They were based at Weymouth, where a flotilla of 200 landing craft and ships assembled in September 1943: He tells the story:

"We started to train those landing craft and ships together with their army cargoes (and also ourselves, as previous training had been to <u>avoid</u> running our ships up a beach) to weld the combined force into a drilled armada capable of hammering a path across the beach defences into Normandy. We mainly used the beaches between

Portland and Poole for practising.

"However, in April 1944 we borrowed Slapton beach for a full scale assault, landing the whole of the 3rd Canadian Division. The Commander of Force J, Commodore Hughes Hallett, had used the lessons learnt at the Dieppe raid in planning for Normandy. He feared that Eisenhower and Montgomery, just returned from the Mediterranean, would not be aware of the more formidable problems posed by the tides of the Channel and the heavily defended French beaches. He wanted to demonstrate his well-practised Plan of Assault to them, the essence of which was to maintain the maximum amount of noise in the beach area from H minus 45 minutes to a crescendo at H minus 1 minute, and then get the infantry ashore and through the beach defences in the next three minutes. So Monty and Eisenhower came to watch this exercise.

"We left from Southampton, simulated the distance of crossing to France, and made for Slapton. It was a good exercise - we had got it to a fine art. Timing was crucial. The general order in which the landing craft attacked the beach can be seen in the following diagram:

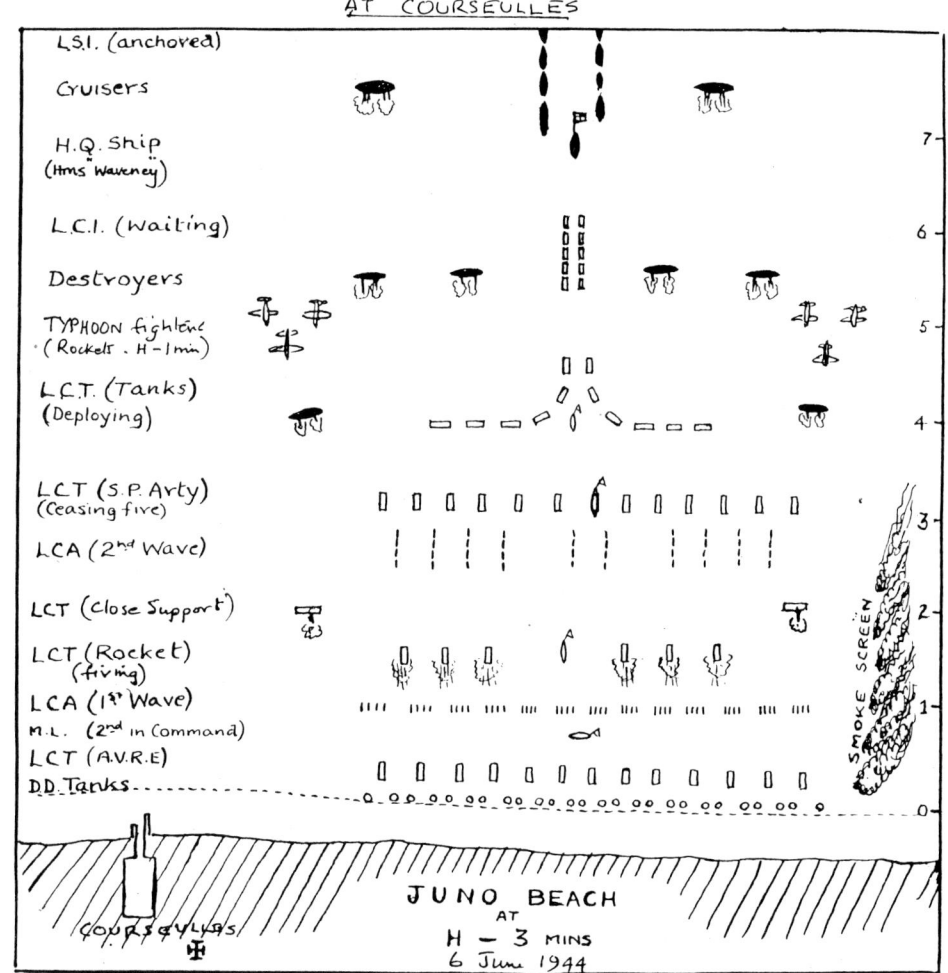

This was the top-secret plan of attack used on D-Day at Juno beach, Courseulles, and rehearsed by the Canadian Force J at Slapton sands in April 1944.

"The first vehicles to reach the beach were the DD (amphibious) tanks, launched from their parent craft some three miles out, to swim ashore at about 3½ knots to settle on the sand with just their gun turret above water at H minus 5 minutes to provide close support for the leading wave of landing craft. The first LCAs carried a weapon called a Hedgerow. It had spigots, two rows, all set at different angles, on each was a small 5 pound bomb. When you discharged the whole lot together they cleared a path up the beach for the big tanks by exploding the mines. The next vehicles off were armoured bulldozers, to clear the obstacles off the beach. That was followed by two flails, to clear any other mines. Next came a Roly Poly, which had a huge bobbin, and unrolled a coir carpet laced with steel to give a grip on the sand. Then came the fascines, i.e. Churchill tanks carrying enormous bundles of twigs about 10 feet in diameter on the front. That went into the ditch, to enable tanks to get across. Last of all was a tank with a huge square plaque of explosives. They clapped this mass of explosives against the wall, went back and exploded it. All this was immediately followed by the Infantry to exploit the breach made in the Great West Wall, as the Germans called it. Cruisers meantime were pounding further inland.

"During the approach phase we had twelve landing craft in line from which the army were firing artillery as they came in. They aimed the guns by aiming the craft. Each craft had 4 howitzers - very effective.

"Afterwards, on the beach, along came Monty and Eisenhower to talk to our Captain, Otway-Ruthven. Monty said he would not have his artillery firing from the landing craft. 'It's a waste of ammunition - I want all that ammunition landed on the beach, not fired before it gets there. You could never be sure of hitting the target.' Otway-Ruthven hit the roof, told him he didn't know what he was talking about, and that the whole assault depended on this. Monty stalked off. To prove our point, another demonstration was laid on at Studland beach to show how accurate and effective that part of the bombardment would be. We succeeded, and Monty enthusiastically changed his mind."

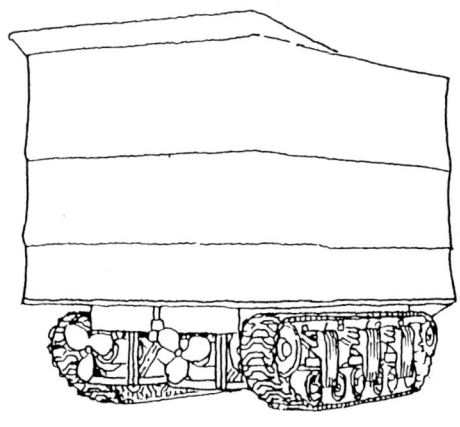

An amphibious tank, which could swim ashore from 3 miles out. One sank near Slapton beach, was salvaged and can now be seen in the car park at Torcross.

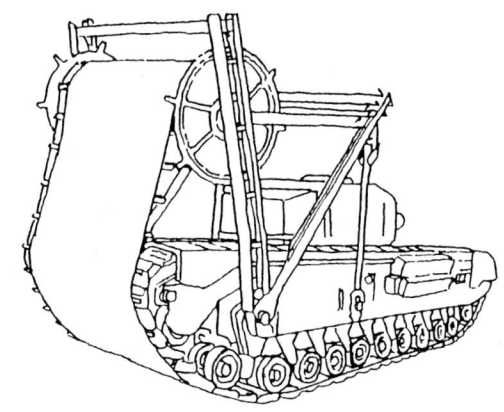

A "Roly Poly" unrolled a coir carpet laced with steel to give tanks and vehicles a grip on the sand.

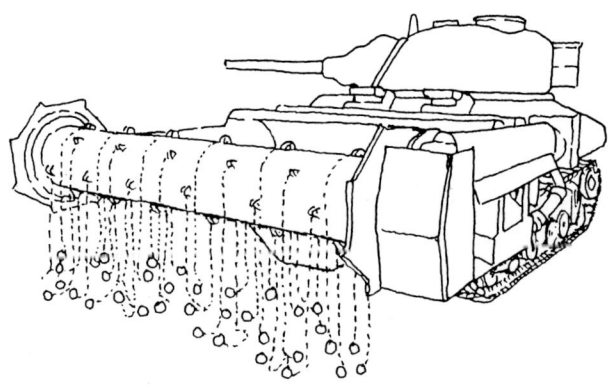

A Flail tank was designed to explode mines to clear the way for troops and vehicles.

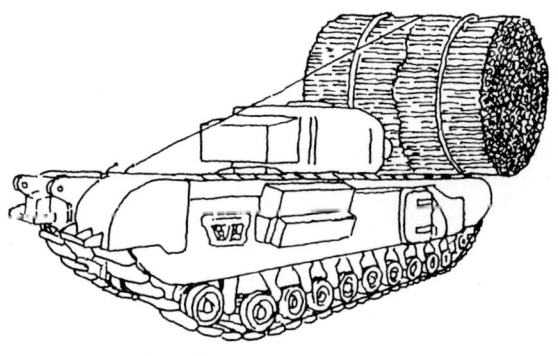

The Fascine tank carried large bundles of twigs which were used to fill ditches to enable tanks to get across.

Chapter 7
Exercise Tiger: April 26-29th, 1944

Several books have recently been published revealing what happened on the ill-fated Exercise Tiger on April 26-29th, 1944.   It was hushed up for years afterwards and, indeed, many who took part in it were at the time quite unaware of the disaster which had occurred.   A diary kept by Maj. Gatling of the American 4th Division describes his experiences.

The plan for this exercise was similar to several held in March and April that year: landing ships and craft left Plymouth, Dartmouth and Brixham fully loaded with men, vehicles and live ammunition and after simulating the crossing to France reached Slapton beach 24 hours later, as planned, on the evening of the 27th. Maj. Gatling was among this first wave of US forces on Capt. Larry Gilbert's crowded LST 282. He wrote in his diary:

"I went off the LST with the men in our 1½ ton truck. We merely followed in convoy in the dark, moving about 3 miles inland to the Division Command Post which had been set up in a farmhouse. We parked our truck in a field, got out our bedding rolls and went to sleep alongside a hedge.   It was drizzling and rather chilly."

Gatling on the next day watched "a number of Long Tom guns which had landed, towed in two parts by enormous prime movers. That afternoon we learned that German E-Boats had attacked and sunk three LSTs the previous night along the coast.   These LSTs were scheduled to land several hours after we had landed. About 700 casualties had been inflicted. The matter was immediately put on a 'top secret' basis."

The 4th Division capture their first German Prisoners

That night, around 2-3 a.m., they heard German planes flying over, in the direction of Plymouth, and anti-aircraft batteries opened up. "We heard one plane coming lower, circling, and obviously in trouble. In a few minutes there was a tremendous crash. Wreckage was strewn over the field for 100 yards. The pilot was killed.   One crew member had bailed out and was captured by our MPs within a few minutes - the first German prisoner captured by the Division. The two other crew members who had bailed out were also captured the following day. One of our interpreters, Cpl. Kleeman, was called upon to interrogate the prisoner for the CIC."

The Tragedy in Lyme Bay

It was Dr. Ralph Greene who first researched and made public the disaster that had happened to the other part of the ships in the exercise.   He had been stationed at Kingswear in March 1944, but by April had been moved to a hospital in Sherborne, Dorset.

On the afternoon of April 28th the doctor in charge of the hospital summoned all the medical officers and nurses and announced: "In less than an hour we'll receive hundreds of emergency cases of shock due to immersion, compounded by explosion wounds. Supreme Headquarters Allied Expeditionary Force demands that we treat these soldiers as though we're veterinarians: you will ask no questions and take no histories.   There will be no discussion.   Anyone who talks about these casualties, regardless of their severity, will be subjected to court-martial. No one will be allowed to leave our perimeter until further orders."

Half an hour later, writes Greene, a stream of ambulances brought in the casualties, - "wet, shivering, blue-skinned, blanketed and bandaged young Army and Navy men.   Before long several hundred men - cold, wet and many in great pain - were being treated inside the hut.   There was no talking......Working in this vacuum, the doctors were gratified that most of the men responded to warmth and 'Tender Loving Care' and large numbers soon could be returned to their units. Many however responded less quickly and despite every effort some died."

Dr. Greene later made it his business to find out what had really happened. It seemed that a second wave of attacking forces had left Plymouth 24 hours after those with Maj. Gatling, in convoy T-4, consisting of eight LSTs to act as a "build-up" to deliver tanks, jeeps, DUKWs (amphibious trucks), all fully loaded with gasoline and explosives. Leading the convoy were intended to be two British warships, HMS Azalea, a corvette, and HMS Scimitar, an elderly destroyer.   Unfortunately HMS Scimitar was rammed by a landing craft in Plymouth harbour, and repairs could not be made in time for her to sail.   Her Captain asked for permission to sail with the hole temporarily plugged, but his request was wrongly routed and did not reach British naval command in time. So the convoy was left guarded only by HMS Azalea and headed, as planned, for Lyme Bay where she was to turn clockwise and simulate the distance of crossing to France before turning back to Slapton.   When the British RN received the delayed message from Scimitar they sent HMS Saladin to replace her, but she did not reach Lyme Bay until 3.15 a.m. on the 28th.

To make matters worse, Comdr. Bernard Skahill USN, the Chief officer of the convoy, had not "obtained copies of the escort orders" and was unaware of the lack of the second guardship. As if that were not enough, "the orders issued to each LST contained a typographical error that gave them the wrong radio frequency on which to communicate with HQ ashore or Azalea. Thus the American ships were unable to get whatever messages would be sent to them en route."

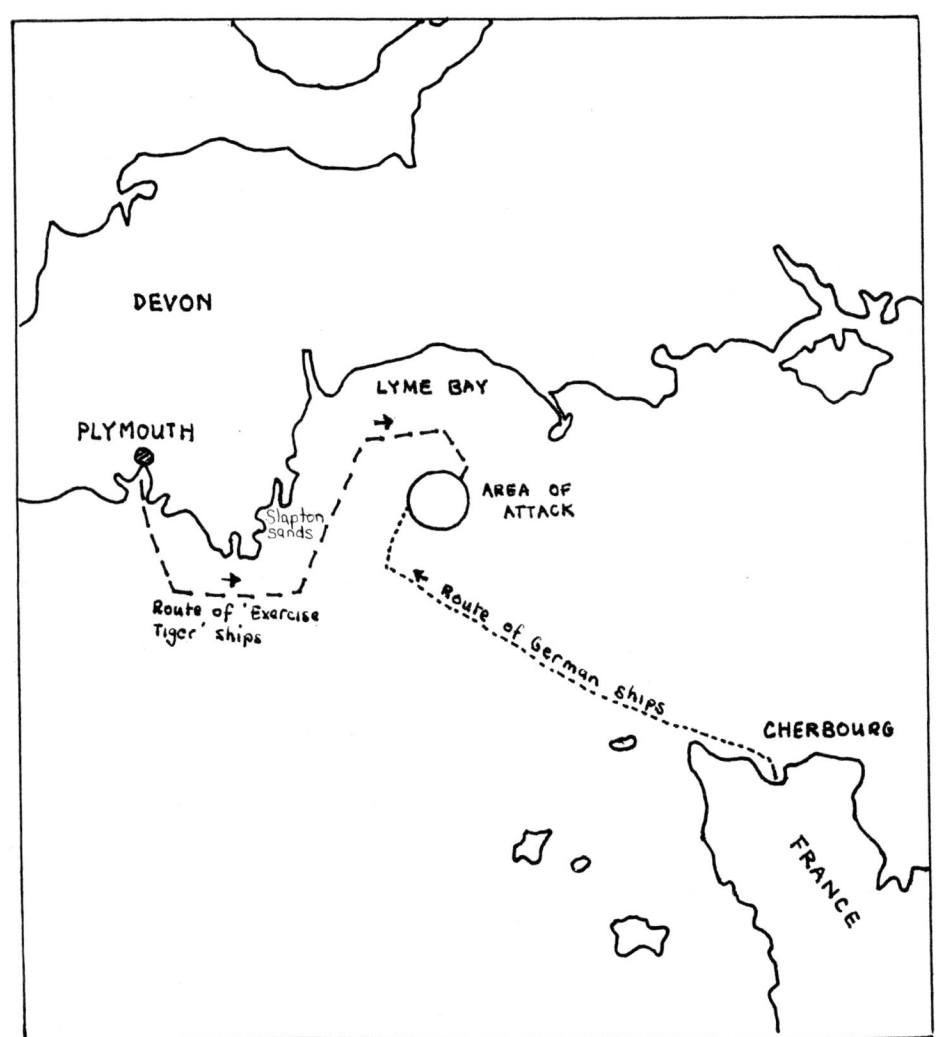

Route taken by Convoy T-4 in Exercise Tiger, and of the German E-boats which attacked them in Lyme Bay, in the early hours of April 28th, 1944.

A flotilla of seven fast German E-boats, carrying torpedoes and cannon, had left Cherbourg that evening under cover of darkness, not knowing about the exercise but having been informed of unusual activity. About midnight they were spotted on radar by HMS Onslow, a destroyer on patrol off Portland Bill, who reported it to Plymouth HQ who, in turn, relayed it to the convoy. Because of the radio mix-up none of the LSTs got the message. At 2 a.m LST 507 was hit by a torpedo and all the vehicles on board loaded with gasoline caught fire. At 2.17, LST 531 was torpedoed and exploded. No lifeboats could be launched and the men were forced to leap into the sea, now covered with a layer of burning gasoline. Hundreds were soon struggling in the chilly waters of the Channel. The Army life jackets which might have saved them had never been tried out before and most men were wearing them round the waist instead of under the armpit. Weakened men were actually pitched forward into the water by them.

HMS Azalea later reported she had seen no E-boats, nor any survivors. HMS Saladin, arriving at 3.15 a.m., did find 50 survivors clinging to LST 507's bow and picked them up. LST 515 's captain, Lt. Doyle, was refused permission to pick up survivors by Skahill but ignored the order despite the danger of his ship being hit. He launched his small landing craft to pick up as many as he could. By dawn, other ships arrived to pick up the bodies and survivors.

The official U.S. toll of dead was 749. However, a recent book by Richard Bass, "Precious Cargo," quoted statements by men of the 146th and 147th Q.M. Co. who on April 28th, on the orders of the 605th Graves Registration Company, took the bodies from near Weymouth, Dorset, to Brookside cemetery in London. They said their trucks carried 1,040 dead, all showing signs of death by drowning or hypothermia. Perhaps the true numbers will never be known. This shows that none of those lost on the two landing craft could have come ashore on Slapton Sands, as is often alleged.

Meanwhile, LST 289 saw the two other craft hit and was zigzagging to avoid the same fate when a torpedo smashed into her stern. However the forward end of the ship was unharmed and the Lt. in charge, despite having lost his rudder, was able to make for Dartmouth where there was a hospital. He had eight missing, four dead on board and another sixteen wounded needing urgent medical aid. Ensign Robert G. Franklin, an American stationed at the Royal Naval College, evacuated his buddy off the damaged LST in Dartmouth harbour.

Brian Ridalls recalls that his father, the pilot, brought her into Dartmouth harbour.

"These LSTs were big ships and had to have a pilot, not like the LCTs which were quite small and came in on their own. The stern was actually blown off. I can remember that. Father tells the story that, as they were coming off, obviously the investigators were going aboard, one chap accidentally kicked something and it was a detonator and it exploded; it hurt his foot. She was alongside the quay opposite the hospital. They were flat bottomed so they didn't draw a lot of water. I think she did go up to Noss to be repaired. I did not see them take the injured off but my Dad did."

Brian Bovey saw it come in too: "After the Lyme Bay exercise this great big landing craft came into Dartmouth with her stern all screwed up. I saw that. The siren went as it was coming in and these young American sailors were diving off the landing craft into the river. They had got so shell-shocked; they had already had one thing; this was all they could think of to do. They got them back on again."

However, all the undamaged LSTs went ahead with the planned assault on Slapton beach, some of them unaware that there had been any disaster. In all, about 200 men were killed in this attack in addition to those lost on the torpedoed landing ships. All those who knew the truth were threatened with court-martial if they talked about it, for fear of damaging morale when the real D-Day came. Security was so tight that among the locals few even heard rumours about what had happened. However, after enquries to establish the causes of the disaster, lessons were learnt. When D-Day came casualties were only a fraction of those suffered in Exercise Tiger.

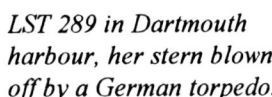
LST 289 in Dartmouth harbour, her stern blown off by a German torpedo.

Chapter 8
The Deception Plan

Maj. General David Belchem in his book, "Victory in Normandy," describes the many efforts to mislead the Germans about the date and targets of the invasion. "The main effort was put into convincing German Intelligence that the principal Allied thrust would be made in the Pas de Calais, sometime in the second half of July."

Several Dartmothians played some part in these deceptions. Richard Davies was one of them. After his training on landing craft at Dartmouth he had been posted to Folkestone. "We were with dummy landing craft, as decoys for D-Day, to fool the Germans that the invasion was going to be on the Pas de Calais. We were there on the actual D-Day."

Lt. Peter Wyatt was on one occasion ordered, with HMS Waveney, to escort a group of landing craft up channel from Portsmouth to Folkestone, to attract the German air force to attack them and make them think that was where the invasion would begin.

Eric Pillar had by now joined the Royal Corps of Signals in a special High Speed Wireless Section manned chiefly by ex-Post Office personnel:

"Prior to D-Day we were part of Patton's Phantom Army. We spent our days transmitting about 20,000 messages a day on the air. We had a bit of a house in Egham, connected by land line to a house in Norfolk and another on the Yorkshire Moors. From this house we used to send messages via these transmitters, totally fake messages about different units, which they would decode, to deceive the Germans. In the Wash in East Anglia they had a lot of fake rubber landing craft and tents and cooker fires going but only a skeleton staff there."

Belchem concludes that the Deception Plan "overall achieved a remarkable degree of success. Hitler and his immediate entourage never seriously wavered in their belief that the main Allied assault would be made in the Pas de Calais until late in July....Hitler continued to regard the Normandy landings as a diversionary operation until it was too late to send effective reinforcements from Fifteenth Army to save Seventh Army from its fate."

Chapter 9
Last days in the Dart: May and early June 1944

The actual date of D-Day was a closely guarded secret, but locals guessed it would be soon. Wren Margaret Blackwell looked out of the window of the train bringing her into Kingswear at the end of April, and noted in her diary:

"There was scarcely room to move on the river. There were craft and ships of all kinds, and so thickly packed were they that one could almost have <u>walked</u> across the river to Dartmouth on the other side. By the look of things the invasion could not be far off."

Temporary Acting Electrical Sub-Lt. Martin Gilbert, RNVR, arrived in Dartmouth on May 14th with G Squadron of 39 Landing Craft Tank, which were attached to Force U, destined for Utah Red Beach. They included two flotillas, of twelve each, of British Mark IV LCTs, and one flotilla of fifteen American design Mark V's. All were sea-going vessels, and their job was to transport American troops, vehicles and tanks across the Channel. Martin describes his job:

"These landing craft were rather like a shoebox, with no bow, nearly 200 feet long and about 20 feet wide. When they were about 200 yards from the beach they would let out a kedge anchor from the stern, so that the LC was always held head to the beach. This was so that the vehicles could land on the beach. After they had landed, there was an electric capstan which was necessary to get the craft off the beach in the shortest possible time. The electric winch was driven by a large motor below the quarterdeck, driven through a gearbox and a vertical shaft nearly ten feet long which went up through the deck. Often these shafts were not very well installed and one of my jobs was to see that every winch was correctly fitted. The other essential piece of electrical equipment was the bilge pump. Any LC landing on the beach makes holes in the bottom, so water starts to come in and if you don't pump it out again you don't make it home. Having landed our troops and vehicles it was essential to get off the beach fast to make room for the next LC."

The fact that with every exercise the landing craft were damaged and had to be repaired explains the frenzied activity along the banks of the river and in the repair shops which worked night and day. No one had any days off and all were short of sleep. Every piece of equipment, much of it temperamental, had to be checked and rechecked to make sure it worked on the real D-Day.

Third Officer Moyra Charlton, WRNS, wrote in her diary on May 25th: "Doran rang me before 8 a.m. to tell me that the flap had come." She was among a group of Wrens working in the Confidential Books (CB) section of HMS Cicala based on the upper floors of the Royal Dart Hotel, Kingswear, and their job was to issue the huge numbers of secret codes and chartlets which came from the Admiralty by courier to the ships. For the next ten days they worked 17 hours a day.

Lt. Peter Wyatt was one of those who had prepared these final orders. Starting with a book of about 350 pages they reduced the orders for each landing craft to one page, which was given to the young Sub-Lt. in charge. Much of it was pictorial, with diagrams, and on the back was navigational information and a photograph taken by the RAF of the section of beach to be attacked. It was about ten days before the actual D-Day that he attended a meeting with all the British chiefs, including Montgomery, at which they learnt exactly where they were going to land and of the whole plan of the Normandy campaign.

Wren Margaret Blackwell in HMS Cicala, who was also one of those who dealt with the distribution of these secret orders, wrote in her diary:

"I knew what it all meant, because I have prepared for landings before, in Gibraltar for the African landings, and in Algiers for the Sicilian and Italian landings...It is one great plan to herd them across the Channel, like sheep to their slaughter.

"And now we see the great landing craft which fill the river packed with men and machines. They lie three and four deep. On they go into the bellies of the great craft. They are like sardines packed in a tin. All just packed, hot,

US Landing Ships 541 and 264 loading up for D-Day from the Embankment, Dartmouth. Vehicles had to reverse onto them.

sweating in the relentless sun.... There are thousands of young American men waiting, cooped up in their ships. They don't want to fight - indeed their forefathers braved a perilous journey across the Atlantic just so that their children might be free from the mad hate and jealousy of Europe."

During late May American forces destined for D-Day had been moved into temporary camps popularly known as "sausages" not far from the coast, where they were confined. By June 1st they were proceeding to their ports of embarkation. Of those who were to leave from the Dart some came by rail to Kingswear station, some by lorry to Maypool, Galmpton and Dittisham. Others arrived on the Dartmouth side. Some Infantry were put into temporary camps on the hills above the town. Local people remember:

"The noise of the truck convoys roaring through the narrow streets, lorry after lorry, loaded with men. They

A loaded Rhino, a large raft fitted with ramps, designed to be joined to the LSTs which could not go in close to shallow beaches. It could take 30 vehicles and 200 men from the ship when 3 miles off shore.

descend down the steep hill, slow down through the town, round the corner, up over the little bridge to the Quays, on and on in an endless number."

Henry C.Moses has his log of LST 281 which states that after practising landings on various beaches they returned to Dartmouth on 12th May. On the 1st June it succinctly recorded "they loaded up with 21 army officers, 336 men; 19 navy demolition unit men, 3 officers; 3 Rhino crew men, 1 officer; 2 medical technicians, 1 officer; 19 tanks, 59 other vehicles."

Maj. Gatling explained that "a Rhino was an assembly of water-tight metal compartments chained together with ramps on top, and an outboard motor on one end." It linked up with the large LSTs which could not get close in to the shallow beaches and enabled them to discharge about 30 vehicles and 200 men onto the Rhino when about 3 miles offshore.

Gatling and his shipload:

"... arrived in Dartmouth about 6 p.m. and drove straight onto LST 282. All the vehicles were parked on the main or downstairs deck, and the men had to sleep either on the vehicles or on bunks set up along the walls. The officers had a cabin with double rows of bunks in groups of three. It was very crowded but we got used to it. There was also on board a large quantity of explosives which we gazed at rather apprehensively until they left the ship with the Seabees early on D-Day."

Ensign John Keffer, USNR, Communications Officer on LST 47.

John W. Keffer was serving on USS LST 47 which put into Dartmouth on May 23rd. He wrote:

"Together with other Communications Officers under the command of Admiral Don Moon, Naval Commander of the Utah Force, I began attending classes in the Royal Naval College to memorise a new code for the invasion. The Normandy beach head had been sectioned off into five areas: Utah, Omaha, Gold, Juno and Sword. The Western Task Force, to which LST 47 belonged, and the U.S. First Army were assigned the Utah and Omaha beaches. Those of us from the five ships constituting the LST assault group destined for Utah Beach were not to be allowed code books aboard for fear of their falling into enemy hands. In order to review the class material I would lock myself in the Communications Office to study...I did not leave the ship for nearly a week. Pre-invasion jitters had begun..."

Cliff Danue on LST 47 recalled: "While we were waiting in the Dart ... the Bridge would be crowded during the 4 to 8 watch with crewmen using the spyglass or binoculars looking toward shore. There was a building there that was the Wren's dormitory and at reveille you could see some interesting sights!"

John Keffer wrote: "On June 1st we pulled up to a hard to commence loading half-tracks, medium tanks and other Army equipment. A Roman Catholic chaplain came aboard to hear confessions and to give us holy viaticum, the Eucharist given to a person in danger of death. The ship was stripped of everything, including personal belongings, not absolutely necessary to the operation of the vessel."

As presumably the chaplains of other denominations were holding similar services aboard the vessels lying in Dartmouth harbour, this suggests they knew that this was not just another exercise.

During these days the locals living on the Dartmouth side in Crowthers Hill, Smith Street, Victoria Road and Duke Street were not allowed out of their houses, but watched through their windows, aware that something momentous was happening. The last to join the landing ships were the infantry camped above the town. With no transport available, they had to walk down, laden with 70 pound packs, and took the shortest way by the hills of Above Town. One eyewitness, Walter Parr Ferris, the local chemist, described them as looking rather like a huge swarm of ants as they came down through the fields and along the narrow streets to the Quay, then across the Royal Avenue Gardens to the Embankment to board their ships.

John Keffer wrote: "On June 2nd we completed loading Army personnel and equipment. As we carried, swinging from davits, six LCVPs, which would transport soldiers to the beach head on D-Day, our commanding officer met with the smallboat coxwains to give them instructions and navigation charts of Utah beach. We

Tanks and trucks being loaded aboard LST 47 for the D-Day embarkation. No more 'dry runs' - this was the real thing.

received aboard 170 crewmen of naval underwater demolition squads, who would set out in rubber craft before H-Hour (even before the small boats headed for shore) with the task of destroying the formidable underwater obstacles the enemy had erected to rip out the bottom of landing ships and craft."

Once aboard, everyone had to wait. Was this to be yet another exercise? Or the real thing? The weather was very hot - for most of May there had hardly been a cloud in the sky. Andrew E. Mercado, on LST 311 recalls killing the time by watching dolphins play in the harbour as they all waited for the orders to sail.

Wren Officer Moyra Charlton, wrote:

"The last of the glorious hot days. I was out on the river all the morning trying to find LCTs and give them their Admiralty bags and envelopes. We went twice up past Greenway House to Dittisham basin. The river was crammed with landing craft filled with American troops. Jazz music splintered the ancient sunny silence of the Dart. Men, stripped to the waist, lay in the sun and shouted to us. Some threw us sweets or gave us last letters to post."

Brian Bovey, aged 13, recalls:

"They were on the decks of these enormous landing craft as if there was no room for them below. They passed the time away while they were waiting blowing up condoms and tying them up and letting them blow away. There were hundreds floating out between the two castles. That was the day before they left."

21

Chapter 10
June 3rd : The Fleet Departs

Wren Margaret Blackwell crossed on the lower ferry to HMS Cicala on the morning of Saturday June 3rd. There was nothing more to do - all the books had been cleared. On the ferry she passed:

"... LSTs and LCTs, large and small, each full of what, at a distance looked like a khaki froth but which when seen close to was a mass of camouflaged men and equipment. Most of the men were basking in the hot June sunshine.

"Then at about mid-day it started. A very large LST ground her way out of the harbour. She had been one of those anchored, tied on to the old rusty iron buoy just outside our office window. She weighed anchor, and out she went. Some of the boys waved to us but not the usual wave of greeting - this was a good-bye wave. And from then on it was one continual stream of landing craft, roaring down the river and out to sea. They never ceased all the afternoon and evening and on into the night."

In all, 485 craft sailed out of the Dart to join the largest amphibious force ever assembled before in history. Gus Sellitto on LST 47 remembers, as they left about 4.00 p.m., the Wrens were on shore signalling by semaphore, "Goodbye and Good Luck!". John Keffer saw this too. He was reflecting that June 5th, which he now knew to be the intended date of D-Day, was also his 21st birthday. Would he survive it?

At sea, a message from General Eisenhower was read:

"Soldiers, Sailors and Airmen of the Allied Expeditionary Force. You are about to embark upon the Great Crusade, toward which we have striven these many months. The eyes of the world are upon you.... Your task will not be an easy one. The enemy is well trained, well equipped and battle hardened. He will fight savagely.... I have full confidence in your courage, devotion to duty, and skill in battle. We will accept nothing less than full victory."

Looking along the crowded deck of an LST loaded with vehicles bound for Normandy, with Dartmouth in the background.

W.A. Corkhill, in the RN, was 18 years old and was on the British LCT 2272 when it left Dartmouth on June 3rd about noon. He believes they had Brigadier-General Theodore Roosevelt, son of the President, and his aides on board.

Staff Sergeant Bernard Krein left Dartmouth aboard an LSI. These large LSIs carried smaller landing craft (LCIs) which were to be launched near to the landing beach. He recalls the tensions among the men involved in facing up to the fact that this was not going to be a "dry run".

"Our dry runs had taken us on the LSIs many times. We knew its gangways, decks fore and aft. There would be no more room for error when the red light went on in the dark hold. We could do it with our eyes closed. Up the 22 steel steps, count them, to the top of the iron grated platform, then step high to clear the murderous door jamb, a fall here could mean a rupture, a broken leg, or worse. Now bend low to avoid the overhanging plates of steel that were put there just to smash our heads in, squeeze through the narrow oblong unbolted hatchway, don't snag your harness on the flywheel of the door. Now, some to the right, some to the left, KNOW YOUR ROUTE TO YOUR LCI, DON'T F*** IT UP NOW..... We had to know where our LCI was moored to the mother ship, where the rope ladder was so as to scramble 30 feet down the side of the ship. UNBUCKLE YOUR HELMET STRAPS. A fall from this height into the sea feet first and the impact of the water into your helmet could break your neck. All our murderous equipment had been prepared and stored in our LCI, all hand made, ready for the killing game.

"Once on the LST we were hurried along the deck to the steel hatch and down into the hold. Every man takes his place and falls into a sitting position, his seventy pound pack eased on his shoulders. The loud hollow clang of the steel doors being shut echoes off the walls of the hull. It is pitch black, not the ghost of a light, the purpose being to accustom our eyes to the darkness when we go topside.

"In the darkness I pondered my fate. Would I be alive tomorrow at this time? ....We must have been down in the hold an eternity when the tension began to ooze from our pores. You could feel it from the sounds of hot breath being expelled and sucked back in. We were all waiting for the first weak link to break and blow his stack, setting us all off, and then it happened, the miracle. From the far dark reaches of the hull came a call, 'caw caw', then somewhere from the right, 'cock-a-doodle-do', over there, 'moo-moo', and then a wild burst of all the barnyard animals imaginable and some not yet invented. Suddenly a commotion from above, the heavy beam of a flashlight piercing the darkness. 'What the hell is going on down there?' The animal calls stop, a five second pause and then laughter.... uncontrollable laughter from one end of the hull to the other. The tension was over, the laughter stopped, we could feel each others' presence, we were going to make it over to the other side, and after that, who knows?"

Krein also recalls that: "On June 4th, the day before the intended invasion, every man was issued with a packet containing a syringe and morphine. 'If you are wounded and can't get help and the pain is unbearable, take a shot of morphine.'"

All the Wrens in Dartmouth were confined to their quarters, escorted by sailors to and from their workplace. This did not stop them from standing on the balconies of the riverside quarters waving to ship after ship as they passed. Wren Blackwell, against orders, walked to the top of a hill on the Kingswear side and looked out to sea.

"The ocean is just crammed with the long low craft as far as one could see. It is as if someone had emptied many boxes of matches into a bowl of water, almost as if one could have walked on them, so close together were they. And on each flank the clear war-like profile of our own cruisers and destroyers could be seen."

The following day, Sunday, she went to the 10.15 Mass at the St. John's Catholic Church in Newcomen Road, Dartmouth. The Priest remarked: "What an ominous silence there is over everything." It hung heavily, and depressed everyone. Margaret Blackwell again walked to the top of a hill:

"Out to sea, on the horizon, the landing craft still bobbed and jostled throughout the day, awaiting zero hour. And during the afternoon the wind rose more and more and a gale warning came through. After all the fine weather we have had, it has to break on this the greatest day perhaps in history!"

Chapter 11
A 24 Hour Postponement

To this vast armada of large and small craft, on the morning of June 4th a message went out that the operation had been postponed for 24 hours. How this affected one typical landing craft is described by Martin Gilbert. He departed on June 3rd with hundreds of other craft on his Mark IV LCT carrying 6 American tanks, lorries and their crews.

"Accommodation on board for the troops was nil - they lived in their vehicles. Only the front end of the LC dropped down, so vehicles had to reverse on - very difficult for tanks. There was a small troop shelter, the width of the deck, containing toilet and washing facilities. It was not intended men should be aboard for longer than 12 hours. One of the lorries carried all the rations for the troops, who were supposed to be self contained. They consisted of K rations, individual packs for one man for two days. They also had A rations, enough for 25 men for one day. They carried enough rations for 26 hours. The RN supplied them with hot tea and coffee. The LC had primitive cooking facilities consisting of a little coal range, to cater for the RN's 14 crew and 3 officers. They had enough food for 7 days, but without a fridge most of it had to be in tins. They had a good supply of whisky and rum however, which they bartered with the Americans for K rations."

Sub-Lt. Martin Gilbert, left, on the landing craft on which he crossed to Utah Red beach on June 6th 1944.

"I had little sleep for many days so, as I had nothing further to do for the moment, I slept most of the way to the assembly point off Weymouth. When I woke up I learnt that because of bad weather D-Day had been postponed for 24 hours, from the night of June 4/5 to that of 5/6. The determining factor was the weather on the far shore. It was not exactly a gale, but severe for landing craft. You cannot land through heavy surf. For sailors the weather was not particularly bad, but the troops were very unhappy. The fact that they were short of food did not worry them as they were all seasick and hardly eating a thing."

Midshipman Tom Griffiths, now living in Dartington, was in HMS Enterprise, a just post-World War I Cruiser which had sailed from Belfast with a considerable force of American, British and French warships. They were ordered to make for the Channel, where they were to take part in bombarding the French coast to back up the landing forces. Midshipmen had to keep a journal, which he still has, and was able to refresh his memory from it. They knew the date planned for D-Day was the 5th June, so on the morning of the 4th they were somewhere off Lands End, intending to reach Portsmouth by the evening and sail straight across to Normandy. However, they received a message to delay everything for 24 hours. So they sailed out into the Atlantic and hung around until June 5th, when they went up Channel. He still recalls:

"One of my most vivid memories on the afternoon and evening of 5th June, when we were in the Channel, was of the incredible number of ships we saw, every way you looked. I am sure I shall never see again so many ships in one place at one time.

"By the evening they were all streaming on prearranged lines. There was a central collecting point - a big area obviously - then the ships fanned out in the five directions for the five main beaches. We went with the American Task Force, to Utah beach. We were doing this bombardment before they actually landed.

"About 1.30 a.m. (on the 6th) we reached the Transport Area and waited there for one hour. Planes were passing over all night and flak was going up from the coast. Strings of flares went down, and hundreds of bombs were hitting and bursting. Parachutists were being dropped behind the coast and the Dakotas returned over us... A little later we wheeled to our Task Force Area and anchored. We were the closest to the beach except for two destroyers who were very close in. There was only four miles of sea between us and France.. For no apparent reason no return fire came from their batteries, though they must have known we were there. The sea was luckily calm and weather conditions looked favourable. At 5.30 a.m. all the ships in the task force, from battleships to landing craft rockets opened fire on targets on the beaches, each with his own target. I know we fired 500 rounds. At 6.30 a.m. the landing craft touched down and we were ordered to cease fire."

Chapter 12
Arrival in Normandy: The Landing

Among the first to land at Utah beach in Normandy were the US Navy Demolition squads. The group of 170 aboard LST 47 set off in rubber rafts even before the LCVPs and headed ashore to blow up the beach obstacles and the roads leading to the landing sites. Don Edwards on LST 47 described these squads as: "The roughest and toughest men I have ever met in my life. They suffered 70% casualties. They figured they were going to die so

they didn't care about anything. Commandos and Rangers were no more than Boy Scouts to that bunch."

Maj. Gatling on LST 282 which was also carrying one of the earliest groups to arrive on Utah Beach. He wrote:

"The Seabee contingent on our ship (about 50 men and officers) left with their explosives in small boats, landing

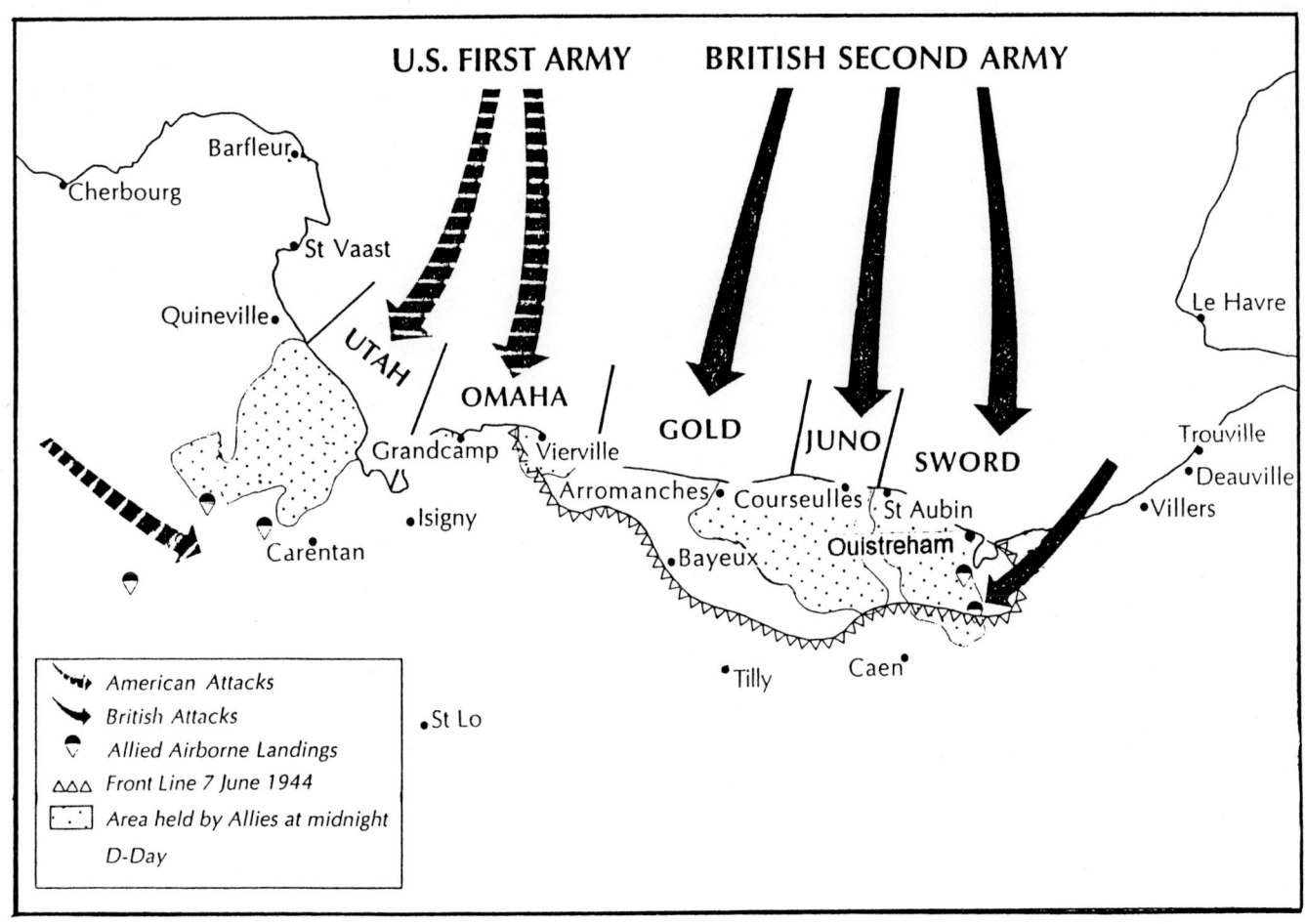

Map of the Normandy beaches, with the area held by the Allies at the end of June 7th, 1944.

craft, etc. between 2 and 3 a.m. and made for the shore... In the early hours of the 6th we heard the airborne troops going over. Their job was to seize certain river crossings and bridgeheads on the Normandy peninsula. At about 4 a.m. the long awaited naval and air bombardment of the coast began. From our LST we could see the whole coastline suddenly lit up in spot after spot as the guns boomed from our battleships and cruisers out at sea. It was vaguely reminiscent of the 4th of July celebrations. As dawn broke slowly we could see the extensive activity of dozens of vessels in the vicinity - LSTs, Transports, LCIs and others. The troops in the leading waves had already gone in for the landing at Utah Beach. However troops on the later waves were being loaded on the smaller landing craft, and artillery, tanks, jeeps and 1½ ton trucks were being loaded onto Rhinos and other smaller vessels."

Meanwhile six LCVPs were lowered into the water from LCT 47 at around 3 a.m., according to John Keffer's log. They headed for Utah beach 12 miles away. Don Flaherty, in charge of one of the boats, described what happened:

"We headed out to the attack transports to load up with Army infantry. We had to travel around 10-12 miles and when we arrived the swells around the transport were about five feet high. Dolan, our Coxswain had a hell of a time holding our boat in close. The soldiers had to climb down the nets into the small boats. If they dropped into the boat when it was going down into a trough they could have broken their legs. If they jumped while the boat was rising on top of a swell they were liable to get crushed between the small boat and the transport. Being loaded down with full packs and equipment didn't make it any easier for them. We finally got them loaded and headed for shore. About half of them got seasick before we hit the beach head. They had each been given small paper bags to vomit into. At the beach they had to jump into ice cold water while being shot at. That morning I was glad I wasn't in the infantry.

"We met up with other boats, formed waves and at H plus 30 we hit the beach where we let the soldiers off. Of the six small boats from LST 47 only two of us were able to get off. The others were either swamped or had their bottoms torn open by the obstacles in the water. All of the fellows eventually got back to the 47.

"Coming off the beach we saw a big explosion about 2,000 yards away: an LST on its way in had hit a mine, and the water was full of debris and men. To get these guys into our boat we had to lower our ramp almost to the water's edge; to keep from swamping and from running over the soldiers, Dolan had to manoeuvre the boat backwards. We were the only boat in the area and these guys were hollering and crying for help. We were able to pull 19 from the water, several went under as we watched but there was nothing we could do. There had been 50 soldiers plus 12 crewmen on the LCT: 43 were lost at that time, the 19 we pulled from the water were the only survivors. Most of them were badly hurt. Every survivor had at least one leg broken; most had compound fractures from the force of the explosion. Several were bleeding from the mouth and nose as a result of internal injuries. Our boat had several medical kits and we administered morphine to some of the men. An Army sergeant from Chicago with a Polish name kept asking for his mother. He died in my arms. We headed for the nearest hospital ship. Once there, they lowered wire baskets in which we placed the men. For them the war was definitely over. That was a scene I shall never forget."

Martin Gilbert had by now crossed the Channel, woken up by someone in the middle of the night who pointed out the aircraft towing the gliders and paratroops across going over the top of the fleet. His LC reached Utah Beach about 10 a.m. as planned. He confirmed that the beach clearance parties had done their job, but he had not witnessed the carnage they had suffered:

"By this time the main assault had been carried out by smaller craft offloaded from the LSTs. We did not see any of this. Each beach had to be cleared by a beach clearance party. In the case of Utah Red Beach, a shallow sandy beach, the obstacles were fairly easy to remove. On some of the rocky beaches they were concreted in and very difficult to remove. By the time we got there, no gunfire was coming in our direction, and the defensive pillboxes were all demolished. I was down below when I heard the winch wire running out, the engines going astern, the crash as the ramps went down, and all the turmoil of the lorries and tanks going out. Their engines had been running for the previous ten minutes. Next thing we were winching off the beach. We beached on a rising tide and floated off about 35 minutes after the vehicles got away. We cleared the beach area as fast as we could and joined up with a returning convoy."

George C. Dirks, a young officer in the US navy, had the reverse of Martin Gilbert's job: on the American LST 377 he was proceeding to Gold beach near Caen, carrying English soldiers. He writes:

"I was in charge of one of the small boats, LCVPs (Landing Craft Vehicle Personnel), which hung by davits, six LCVPs to each LST, which would be launched and loaded with British soldiers from a troop carrier and ferried from the carrier to the beach.

"It was a foggy cold morning as we ploughed across the water. The hundreds of LSTs proceeding towards the five beach heads on the French coast seemed like toy boats, suspended by cables from the sky. The ships each had a helium-filled balloon floating above them, tethered to the ship by a cable, to protect the ships from being strafed by German aircraft. As we made our way no planes flew out to strafe us. We thought this wasn't so bad, as we dropped anchor and prepared to launch our six LCVPs. As we came in range a heavy barrage of fire from German tanks on shore opened up against our ships. We knew then this was the real thing. Although we had spent many days practising landings on beaches back in Florida we had never known anything like this. Unbelievable noise and explosions were everywhere. The beaches were mined and we were under heavy enemy fire from the shore.

Examples of beach obstacles, attached to mines, erected by the Germans to hinder Allied landings along the entire Atlantic coast.

A painting by Com. Dwight Shepler, USNR, of the bombardment of Utah Green Beach with landing craft going ashore, on June 7th, 1944.

"Our practice rehearsals did pay off, because we seemed to respond to the terrifying chaos in a routine manner. As I manoeuvred my LCVP and circled towards the troop carrier I felt a little safer with the realization that the German tanks were not shooting at our small boats, they were trying to hit the larger ships. We would load up, make it to the beach, unload, and then circle back, forming a sort of line, taking turns, and repeating the process over and over. Shells thundered overhead. Before long, the beach was partially cleared of obstacles but there were still dangerous obstructions to avoid. Enemy aircraft soon took over, but they too were not concerned with small boats like ours; they concentrated on the big ships. It was a tense situation before the German tanks were destroyed and the troops could move forward and move out the Germans from their bunkers along the shore."

Major Gatling off Utah beach wrote:

"Around noon, a Rhino was fixed to our vessel, and it took about 30 vehicles with 200 men and officers ashore. We took off from the LST about 1330 and started slowly in towards the beach about three miles distant. The weather was still overcast, but the visibility was fairly good. There were a multitude of small boats and landing craft, some on the way in and others returning. Wounded were already being ferried across the English Channel.

"When our Rhino got 200 yards from the shore we could see that shells were coming in fairly regularly and seemed to be coming closer down to the water's edge. The men and vehicles who had landed from a couple of landing craft a little ahead of us were scattered out, and 'hit the dirt' regularly when the shells came in. One vehicle was hit and completely destroyed. When we were perhaps 100 yards from the water's edge we hit solid ground. The water was shoulder high. Our first vehicles started down the ramp of the Rhino towards the shore. Some got through and others 'conked out' in the water and could only wait until the little bull dozer could come and drag it ashore. The shelling was getting closer and one or two shells landed 75-100 yards away. Lt. Col. Bryant, senior officer on our Rhino, ordered the men to walk on into the shore and try to find cover beyond the stone wall, with only the driver staying with the vehicles. When our 1½ ton truck went down the ramp all the men had preceded it on foot. I waded on, the water up to my neck and followed the truck. It went a little distance and then stopped in about four feet of water. The driver immediately got to work on it."

Maj. Gatling waded ashore and went to look for the rest of his men, seeing on the way the body of one American. Shells were landing all round. He found a number of German prisoners, most of them wounded, and finally went back to find the truck. Its driver had miraculously restarted its engine and driven it ashore.

"We were all soaking wet, and our equipment too...I hopped on board and we tried to locate the main exit road off the beach. There was so much traffic, but we finally got off the beach, being careful to stay in the tracks of previous vehicles for fear of buried mines. The road ran through a breach in the wall and along a sort of causeway across a wide inundated area that we had seen in aerial photos. Not far along the causeway we saw several of our tanks which had been knocked out... We went inland about a mile to the Divisional Command Post near a little place called Ste. Marie du Mont. It was clustered about a farmhouse, and we parked the truck in a field....It was about 5.30 p.m and we got out our K rations and went to work with supper.

"This farm was entirely undamaged and was about as peaceful looking as it if were a thousand miles away from the war. The farmer seemed to be going about his business with his children as assistants without visible anxiety, keenly watched by the soldiers sitting around on the ground and vehicles. There were cows, pigs, donkeys, chickens, ducks, goats, geese, cats, dogs and rabbits much in evidence. I shall never forget that peaceful pastoral scene at my first stopping place in France."

Meanwhile John Mee, now of Dartmouth, then a Staff Sergeant in the British Royal Artillery, was 1st pilot of a glider carrying 28 men of the Royal Corps of Signals being towed by an Albemarle bomber towards the French coast in the early afernoon of June 6th. He recalls:

"We landed without damage about four miles behind the British Sword beach, Ouistreham, just clearing a stone wall and missing the anti-landing poles set up by the Germans. There were about 200 gliders coming over at this time in our section. We shook hands with the Signals men and wished each other good luck. I and the second pilot had been told to get to the nearest beach where we would be picked up and brought back to England. The glider could not be recovered but pilots had to be used for more runs. We had no idea of the military situation, so kept under cover hiding in hedges as we made for the coast. We slept in a ditch that night, hearing a lot of sniper fire from the Germans although we could not see them. When we reached Sword beach it was covered with dead bodies, mostly Germans but many British as well, and there was the smell of death everywhere. Landing craft were coming in all the time bringing more troops. I thought: 'Poor souls, what a sight to greet them.' How lucky I was to be taken back to England in one of those ships."

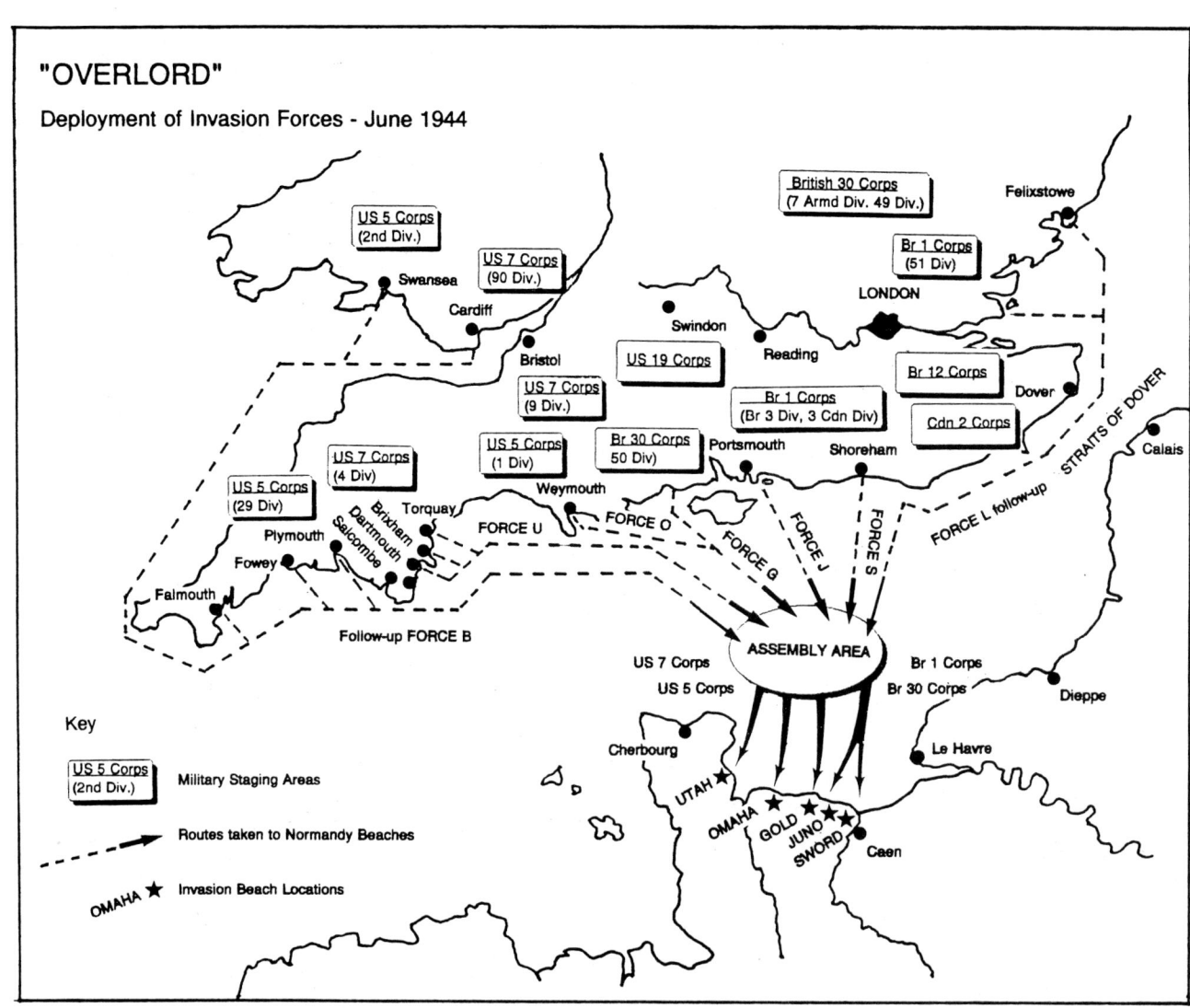

Map of Southern England, the Channel and the French coast, showing the location before D-Day of the military units which took part in Operation Overlord.

Some LSTs were soon being used to ferry Allied wounded and German prisoners of war back to England. Warren Ambrose on LST 283 wrote:

"We landed on Utah beach on D-Day carrying a Ranger unit which was supposed to slip through the lines and head up the peninsula for Cherbourg. After putting the troops ashore we turned our ship into a hospital ship and took on casualties. We headed back for England, picked up reserve troops and made for to Omaha beach. There we took on a load of prisoners, and were surprised to find they were Polish troops who hated the Russians more than the Germans since they came from Eastern Poland. All in all we made 9 trips to Normandy before we were ordered to the Mediterranean."

John Keffer on LST 47, after landing troops on Utah beach, also records carrying prisoners:

" On our first return voyage to England on June 10th, we transported the first German prisoners from Utah beach, numbering 1,000 men and one French woman, a prostitute!. Ours and other ships transporting German prisoners earned the nickname of 'Herring Fleet' because we were bringing back to England a catch of 'Herrenvolk.'"

Casualties on June 6th at Utah beach were 200 dead - probably less than a tenth of those suffered in Exercise Tiger. Those who attacked Omaha beach were not so lucky. The American Vth Corps there suffered 2,000 casualties, dead and wounded. However, the Allied High Command had feared many more might be lost in order successfully to establish troops ashore on that first day.

Mulberry Harbour

A vital requirement as soon as the troops were ashore was that they could be supplied regularly from ships at the sea, and for this a safe harbour was required. Sub-Lt. Dick Moger, RNVR, who had been a trainee manager at Philip's shipyard before the war, was on a large ocean

Mulberry Harbour, off Arromanches, seen from the air. The caissons from which it was made were towed across the Channel and sunk, along with a few old vessels as blockships, to provide a breakwater. Inside this, a second line of caissons was linked to the shore by floating pontoons, enabling trucks carrying supplies to be driven ashore. Although badly damaged by storms soon after it was built, it was repaired and played a vital part in the Allied victory.

going tug, Growler, which had a few months earlier been given the task of towing from Liverpool to Selsey Bill one concrete caisson of what was later to be Mulberry Harbour. This was the first of many taken to the Portsmouth area ready for the invasion, whence they were towed across to Arromanches, and sunk to form a harbour.

On the actual night of the invasion Dick Moger's tug, Growler, towed across an old French warship dating from around 1900, the Corbière, complete with her four ring French Captain, officers and crew, which was sunk near the entrance to Caen to form a breakwater. Growler was supposed to bring the French officers and men back to Portsmouth afterwards.

"However, the French Captain came to the Captain of Growler and said: 'I need to go ashore. I need to send some soil of my beloved France to De Gaulle, Churchill and President Roosevelt.'

"Nobody from ships was allowed ashore - the army had far too much going on to have a few extra people wandering around. But the French Captain was of senior rank to Growler's, so he felt he'd better do what he wanted. He called the motor boat away and the boatscrew took our captain and the French captain ashore. Because of the gently shelving beach it was not possible to get the boat close enough in for the French captain to land without getting his feet wet. So he climbed onto the back of one of our sailors and was carried ashore! He then dug up some sand, put it into separate bags and came back to the tug. We next had to transfer the rest of the French crew onto the tug and take them back to Portsmouth. By this time at least 25% of them had pushed off - they had gone ashore. They must have swum, there was no other way they could have gone. They weren't going back to Portsmouth when they were so near their own homes and families. So we took the rest of them back.

"While we were lying beside the Mulberry harbour off Arromanches there were some battleships there bombarding the shore. We went alongside HMS Rodney, when I was on the bridge. Suddenly, from high above me on the deck of Rodney came a voice: 'Cor bugger, Dick, what are you doing here?' I looked up and saw it was Bill Woodgate of Dartmouth, who had been an apprentice shipwright at Philip's at the same time as I was a trainee manager."

"The next thing we did was Force Pluto - the Pipe Line Under the Ocean. We went to Cherbourg with three other tugs. Pluto looked like a vast cotton reel with two ice cream cones stuck on each end. The tugs towed from the ends of the ice cream cones. There was one tug each side, the third tug was a little one which steered it and kept it straight. There were 72 miles of pipe and you had to keep on course or you might run out of pipe. It had to end up on a carpet of steel laid in Sandown Bay in the Isle of Wight. We just made it: as we sailed into Sandown Bay between the buoys, out popped the end, and we were left with a cotton reel with nothing on it."

Also near to the Mulberry Harbour was Eric Pillar, with his High Speed Wireless Section equipment to transmit news back of the progress of the invasion. His group went over on a small landing ship on the afternoon of D-Day.

"We weren't intending to land as we had some static wireless equipment and the war-correspondents' copy was very late to us from ashore. We transmitted it back to this country to the Post Office station. It was high speed wireless which is done by tape. We transmitted about 120 words a minute. It had a machine like a typewriter which you type in and it comes out on a tape with holes in Morse. Then it goes through an automatic Morse key, and in England on the receiving station another automatic thing like a pen put the Morse signals on tape. You sit down at a typewriter with the tape in front of you and transcribe it. We were transmitting the correspondents' copy. On board the ship we had our own censors to make sure they didn't say anything they shouldn't. These were the stories which appeared in the newspapers day by day."

Though outside the scope of this account, the later exploits of some of these LSTs and LCTs used in the Normandy invasions should not be forgotten. Many of them, including LSTs 283 and 47, soon sailed to the Mediterranean to take part in landings in the south of France. Richard Davies and Jim George went on their much smaller LCTs to the recapture of Singapore and Rangoon. John Keffer on LST 47 went to the Pacific to invade Okinawa in May 1945, and in September that year was part of the first convoy to arrive in Tokyo Bay after the defeat of Japan.

POSTSCRIPT
Back in Dartmouth, June 5/6th, 1944

Wren Third Officer Moyra Charlton and her friend walked out on the Kingswear side of the river about midnight on June 5/6th and HEARD GUNS VERY LOUD AND CLEAR ACROSS THE SEA. Strangely enough Wren Margaret Blackwell heard them too, on the Dartmouth side even at her Wren quarters in Broadstones, also at about midnight. She wrote that they went off and on spasmodically all night, shaking the windows and the house. Leading Wren Joyce Corder, going to work at the College at 6.30 on the morning of the 6th, also heard them. All of them rushed to listen to the early morning news bulletin, which spoke of German reports of Allied paratroops in Normandy and Cherbourg. At 9 p.m. Churchill confirmed the story and said that in all branches our losses have been relatively small.

Those evacuated from their homes in the South Hams might have thought they could soon move back home, but it was not until the following November that they were allowed to return, sadly to find their homes wrecked and their fields filled with unexploded bombs.

Tom Griffiths reports a curious coincidence. "In 1985 one of the grandsons of F.D.Roosevelt was made Principal of the Dartington College of Arts. As I also worked in the College and had been in America we got on quite well. One day I noticed in his office a shell case that had been made into an ashtray. On it there was an inscription: "Presented to F.D.Roosevelt, President of the United States of America, on the occasion of his birthday, 1945, spent on Tuscaloosa. This shell was fired on D-Day." I recollected that probably I had heard that shell fired on D-Day, as Tuscaloosa was never more than two miles from us. I had not realised that FDR spent his last birthday in this world on board the Tuscaloosa."

ACKNOWLEDGMENTS

The Dartmouth History Research Group would like to thank the Washington Archive, Dartmouth Museum and Britannia Royal Naval College for allowing the use of pictures and photographs in this booklet, and the people listed below who have provided taped memories, diaries, letters, personal photographs and other documents. The painting reproduced on the front cover was by Com. Dwight Shepler, USNR, as were two others used in the text. We are very grateful to Henry H. Milllman whose son published our appeal for U.S. memories in the Miami Herald, which resulted in much material being sent to us, and to John Keffer who has provided us with extracts from "I Remember", a collection of memories by those who served on LST 47. We especially thank Mrs Wanda Manktelow by whose efforts in the U.S. so many veterans of Dartmouth's D-Day were put in touch with us.

Residents of Dartmouth, Kingswear, Dittisham and the South Hams:

Brian Bovey, Mrs R. Biscombe, Peter Clare, Mrs Dawson, Walter Parr Ferris, deceased, Reg and Sheila Little, Basil Mitchelmore, Mrs Pearl Mitchelmore née Rogers, Jean Parnell, Eric and Jessie Pillar, Brian Ridalls, Dick Rushton, Mrs G. Plowright, Mrs Freda Widger, Miss M. Wotton.

British Servicemen and Women:

Margaret Blackwell, Leading Wren, deceased; Moyra Macleod née Charlton, 3rd Officer WRNS; Leading Wren Joyce Corder; W.A.Corkhill, RN; Richard Davies, Coxswain, RN; Jim George, Coxswain RN; Martin Gilbert, Sub-Lt. RNVR; Tom Griffiths, Mid. RN; John Mee, Staff Serg. Glider Pilot, R.A; Dick Moger, Sub-Lt. RNVR; Leo Radford, RAF; Bill Woodgate, RN; E. Webber, RN; Capt. Peter Wyatt, CBE DSC RN, then Lieut.

In US Navy and Army:

Ambrose, Warren L. 832 Live Oak Dr., Angels Camp, Cal. 95222. — On LST 283, at Utah and Omaha beaches.

Berkowitz, I.R. 3600 Mystic Pointe Dr. # 1009 Tower 300 Aventura, FL 33180 — "K" Co. 16th Infantry 1st Inf. Div.

Bradley, Francis X. 157 Woburn St. Medford, MA 02155 — Editor of "The Leaves" official publication of of 4th Inf. Div. Assoc.

Clemesha, W.D. 10970 S.W. 171st Terr. Miami, FL 33157-4006 — British, lives in Miami At school in Dorset 1944.

Danue, Cliff — On LST 47 in Dartmouth and at Utah Beach. Quoted in "I Remember."

Dirks, George C. 1555 Cherry St. # 11 San Carlos, Cal. 94070 — On LST 377, carried British soldiers to Gold beach.

Dosch, Theron R. (Rudy) 6466 S. Brentwood Way Littleton, CO 80123-3514 — On LST 345 in R. Dart, went to Gold beach.

Edwards, Don K. 7790 State Rd, Cincinnati, Ohio 45255 — Radioman 2/c on LST 47, left Dartmouth for Utah beach. Quoted in "I Remember."

Flaherty, Don — On LST 47 in R. Dart. Landed US troops on Utah beach D-Day. Quoted in "I Remember."

Franklin, G. Robert (Bob) 1101 River Reach Dr. Ft. Lauderdale, FL 33315 — Stationed at Naval College, Dartmouth. Bomb Disposal. Ensign, later Lt. J.G.

Gatling, Col. Norbonne P. (Diary quoted by kind permission of his son.) — Dec., Maj. in 4th Div. D-Day, later Col. Left from Dartmouth, on Utah beach from LST 282 D-Day.

Gilbert, Larry E. 2630 W.E. 7th Pl. Homestead, FL. 33033 — In 4th Div., C.O. of LST 282, carried 1st two Assault Waves to Utah Beach on D-Day.

Glass, Nap. 20500, W. Country Club Dr. #602 Aventura, FL 33180 — Involved in preparations for D-Day, got to France afterwards.

Hildebrand, Frank — Deceased 1991. Sister Jane Greer, 400 Longbrook Way, # 229 Pleasant Hill, CA 94523, asks where he sailed from in 981st ORD. DEPOT CO.

Keffer, John W. 2, St. James Place, London SW1A 1NP — Ensign, Communications Officer on LST 47. Left Dartmouth on June 3rd. At Utah beach D-Day.

Kleeman, Werner 45-46 196th Pl. Flushing, NY 11358 — Cpl. and Interpreter in 4th Div. on LST 282, left Darmouth June 3rd for Utah Beach on D-Day.

Krein, Bernard, 17092 Collins Ave. #C-504, Sunny Island, FL 33160-3606 — Staff Sergeant in 8th Inf., 4th Div. left from Dartmouth, in first wave on Utah beach.

Mercado, Andrew E. P.O.Box 175 Nice, CA 95464 — In USN, on LST 311. Left from Dartmouth June 3rd for Utah beach on D-Day.

Millman, Henry H. 1301 East Long St. Carson City, Nev 89706 — On LST 308, left Dartmouth June 3rd for Juno beach.

Moses, Henry C. 4 Upland Rd Weekapaug, R.I.01891 — On LST 281, Executive Officer. Has ship's log. Left Dartmouth June 3rd for Normandy

Remedio, Dominick P. 291 Atlantic Isles N. Miami Bch, FL 33160 — U.S. Army Master Sgt. Left on June 3rd in LST, 13th wave, for Normandy beach.

Sellito, Gus — Storekeeper 3/c on LST 47, left Dartmouth for Utah beach June 3rd. Quoted in "I Remember."

Shapiro, Isadore 17232 S.W. 113th Ct. C Miami, FL 33157 — 4th Inf. Div. Military Police on Utah beach. Kept troops moving.

For background information the following books have been consulted: Maj. David Belchem, "Victory in Normandy;" Edwin P. Hoyt, "The Invasion Before Normandy;" Dr. Ralph Greene and Oliver Allen, "What Happened off Devon" (American Heritage Feb. 1985) and Richard Bass, "Precious Cargo," 1993.